How

Through Tough
Times and Come
Out Victorious

Powerful Promises and Encouragement
from God Backed by Biblical Scriptures
for Difficult Situations.

Gedaliah Shay

Table of Contents

INTRODUCTION 1

Chapter 1 4

Chapter 2 12

Chapter 3 19

Chapter 4 24

Chapter 5 29

Chapter 6 34

Chapter 7 39

Chapter 8 44

Chapter 9 48

Chapter 10 56

Chapter 11 67

Chapter 12 72

Chapter 13 79

Chapter 14 86

Chapter 15 90

A Prayer for Hard Times 104

INTRODUCTION

Offer the sacrifices of righteousness, And put your trust in the Lord.
There are many who say, Who will show us any good? Lord, lift up the light of Your countenance upon us. Psalm 4:5-6.

Tough times can never but come, everyone at one point or the other will experience it. This time is not to break you but to make you stronger.
The essential thing is to learn a lesson which would become an experience for you to tackle any difficulty in the future. Life itself is like an examination hall. You would be tested with what you know and for what you know. If you truly understand the life lessons, you would

1

overcome and receive more authority in life.

No student wants a promotion and runs away from the examination. Indeed, difficult times which is like a life examination are never sweet moments. However, it will interest you to know that nothing precious comes without a price. Your price to your desire Haven is the difficulty you may be experiencing now.

The juice in the orange only comes out through pressing. The only way to win in life is by fighting to win. As a believer, you have a winning mindset, that's why the end product of that battle for you is praise and victory.

This book is set to give you a leap from your present level. Read with all of your heart till something happens on your inside, which will bring about the desired results which you seek.

To your victory!

Chapter 1

TRUSTING GOD IN DIFFICULT
TIMES

Trust is an absolute dependence on
something or someone. Before you trust
someone, you must have seen his ability
in that which you are trusting Him. For
example, you can trust someone to
deliver building materials for a project,
and you will be sure he would deliver it
well. Why? Because he had done it for
you before, he was tested and now can be
trusted.

The ability of God is far beyond what can
be compared to any. The Bible is full of
several promises of God to mankind. The

testimonies of men and women God had dealt with, and those who had dealings with God are strong enough for you to see how God operates. Those testimonies were written for your faith and trust in God. If God did it for them He will do it for you, the reason is that he does not change and does not lie.

God is not a man, that He should lie, Nor a son of man, that He should repent. Has He said, and will He not do? Or has He spoken, and will He not make it good? Numbers 23:19

God does things in a way that supersedes the thought of man. It takes spiritual understanding to trust him, not just your human understanding because your

5

knowledge will fail you. To trust God, you need to look beyond the physical. You will need to take your eyes off the natural phenomenon. See what the scripture says:

Trust in the Lord with all your heart, And lean not on your own understanding; In all your ways acknowledge Him, And He shall direct your paths. Do not be wise in your own eyes; Fear the Lord and depart from evil. Proverbs 3:5-7.

You need to know that, the Lord is aware of your situation or whatsoever you are going through. Whether difficult or not. Nothing is unknown to Him. Though He is mindful of your case, you need to come to God and reason with Him. God expects that all His children come to fellowship with Him first, then in that fellowship, you can table your request what you will have Him do for you.

Come now let us reason together... Isaiah 1:18

Some Christian believers today, don't trust God for anything. Once it's not happening the way they want they seek another way which is against the will of God; no wonder why some have untold pains and anguish that could last for the rest of their lives unless God shows mercy. Whenever you are about to take a decision, no matter how small the situation may be, go to God and talk with

Him. He will reveal to you if you trust Him enough because the way you think is right might be a wrong path.

There is a way that seems right to a man, But its end is the way of death. Proverb 16:25

PRAYERLESSNESS IS PRIDE AGAINST GOD

If there is a man who genuinely trusts in the Lord, that man must be a man of prayer. He must commune with God day in day out just like King David.

Evening and morning and at noon I will pray, and cry aloud, And He shall hear my voice—psalm 55:17.

Prayer is communication with God, our creator. It is a means of transaction between God and man. If a man can pray, then God is always there to answer. Get this right; you don't only pray when you are in need, you pray because that is the lifestyle God expects you to live.

It is also important to know how to pray correctly. No one can school you on how to pray but the Spirit of God. You have to depend on the personality called the Holy Spirit. The challenge we have today, why many believers are doing things wrongly, in their way is lack of dependence on the Spirit of God.

Jesus said in one of His teachings, *"it is expedient for me to go so that the Spirit of truth will come and guide you into all truth"*

However, when He, the Spirit of truth, has come, He will guide you into all truth; for He will not speak on His own authority, but whatever He hears He will speak; and He will tell you things to come. John 16:13.

There is a truth about your life that will bring the joy, the progress and help you need which only the Spirit of God can reveal to you. It would not just come unless you are given to much of prayers.

If you are truly trusting God who never fails, give yourself to prayer. That difficulty will give way as you persist.

Chapter 2

KEEPING HOPE ALIVE

You might have been through a lot.
Probably, storms of life almost swept you
off your feet. You might have been
through numerous days of weeping,
sadness and mourning, days you felt like
giving up. I even heard you almost
committed suicide. Remember!
Weeping may endure for a night, but joy
comes in the morning.

Keep hope alive!
Rejoice again!
Don't give up!

Your time of rejoicing isn't far from here.

It is your time to laugh.

Many who laughed you off will come to rejoice with you.

You are God's delight. No man can steal your joy unless you permit him.

Obed in the bible was called a man of sorrow, but he refused to dwell on the status quo. He challenged the status quo by going to the one who created him. He prayed that his life experience a turnaround and God changed his story. He kept hope alive, and God showed up.

There is a common saying that, *"When there is life, there is hope"*.

Yes, since you still breathe in and out, don't give up on yourself. Don't write off your situation. People who write off a man who is still living should be pitied because they do not have an idea of what can happen to him in a second. Never you write off a man who is still alive. In the twinkling of an eye, his story can be changed that all who have known him will stand in awe.

You will still get that dream job. You will carry your baby if you refuse to believe the doctor's report. You can get your dream spouse if you do not write yourself off.

Get up today and wipe out your tears. Shake off sadness. Throw away that thought of committing suicide. As long as you are breathing, don't give up. There is light at the end of the tunnel.

Very soon, people will gather to celebrate with you. Those who have mocked you shall surround your table to rejoice with you.

He was mocked by his friends when he was undergoing a hard time. His friends asked him to curse God so he could die. Job didn't consent. He trusted in God for his deliverance even when all things fell apart for him.

When Job experienced a turnaround, his latter end was greater than his beginning. He regained in hundreds of folds what he had lost. His friends who had written him off came to celebrate him because he's lifting was undeniable.

Now the Lord blessed the latter days of Job more than his beginning; for he had fourteen thousand sheep, six thousand camels, one thousand yokes of oxen, and one thousand female donkeys. Job 42:12

There is hope for a tree, even though it is cut off, it shall sprout again.

Laugh!

It is your time.

Your appointed time to rejoice.

Hope again.

YOU CAN EXPERIENCE PEACE IN THE STORMY SEA

When Peter was drowning in the stormy sea, there was someone who made a

declaration that calmed the sea. That
person is Jesus.

*These things I have spoken to you, that in
Me you may have peace. In the world you
will] have tribulation, but be of good
cheer, I have overcome the world. John
16:33.*

In this world, we will have tribulations,
but the father has given us an assurance
that we are more than conquerors;
therefore, we can't be moved.
If Jesus is in your boat, even if the storm
rages, He will speak and tame it. Woe is
unto a man who puts his confidence in
another man. There is only one name
under the heavens by which a man can be
saved, and that's the name of Jesus.

It doesn't matter what you are going through; it doesn't matter what you have gone through. Just rest in Jesus.

Sometimes, things may not go as planned, and it may even look like there is no God. In such a time as this, there is only a man that could calm the storm, I have seen him done this countless times. That's Jesus.

Yield your all to Him. Submit to His Lordship. Storms hear him. Waves of the sea obey him. He made them all.

Henceforth, entertain no fear any longer. The one who calms the sea is in control.

Chapter 3

WHEN GOD IS SILENT

I waited patiently for the Lord; And He inclined to me, And heard my cry. Psalm 40:1

There are times you are going through a challenging situation; you are calling on God for help and seems as if He is silent. In such a situation you may be worried and almost discouraged, but I want you to know that God is never silent but working out something bigger than what you are praying for.

You need to know how to wait upon God, even though it may not be as easy as anyone thinks. You are the only one who knows what you are going through, no other person could feel the heat, but Jesus knows about it. He is touched by your infirmity. He was once here, and He knows what it means to feel pain.

For we do not have a High Priest who cannot sympathize with our weaknesses, but was in all points tempted as we are, yet without sin. Hebrew 4:15.

What you are going through He had been through it before and overcame, so you can depend on Him. There is need for you to wait.

When you are seeking God, and it seems as if he is silent, He is not truly silent, but His silence has a meaning; *I have perfected this, you will soon see the result.*

Don't get discouraged. Continue the excellent work you are doing. Something extraordinary is being prepared for you. You would soon see beyond what you are praying for. All your desires are about to become tangible.

GOD SPEAKS IN SILENCE

And after the earthquake a fire, but the Lord was not in the fire; and after the fire a still small voice. 1King 19:12.

You need to learn how to hear the silent voice of God. No matter the silence, God is still communicating certain things to us.

I want you to know that as you go to God worshipping and later presenting your case to Him, He will hear you; he can listen to the most minute word in your heart unuttered.

Never assume God does not hear your prayer because you have not heard him speak to you. God may use signs to communicate with you. He may just put peace in your heart. What about joy? It's another sign God put in your heart to make you know He has heard you and working out some things for you.

Sometimes, God may decide to send someone to you to help you understand and confirm His communication to you at that time. God never watched His children pray and seeking without any response. I believe God is set to do the unimaginable in your life. Watch it!

Chapter 4

STRENGTH IN MY WEAKNESS

And He said to me, My grace is sufficient for you, for My strength is made perfect in weakness. Therefore, most gladly I will rather boast in my infirmities, that the power of Christ may rest upon me. 2 Corinthians 12:9

Human strength is limited, compared to God's power. No matter how strong you are, there is a time your strength will fail you, and it will be as though you have been drained of your strength by 40 days of dry fasting. Now, get this right I'm talking about physical, emotional and spiritual strength.

The most important of them is your spiritual strength. When your spiritual strength is intact, it can affect other types of strength positively.

The spirit of a man will sustain him in sickness, But who can bear a broken spirit? Proverb 18:14.

With spiritual strength, you can turn your emotional and physical weaknesses into strength.

WHAT SHOULD YOU DO WHEN YOU ARE WEAK?

If you faint in the day of adversity, Your strength is small. Proverb 24:10

When you are weak, you need strength, and the only source of power is God. The reason people commit suicide is a lack of knowledge. Your knowledge of God brings strength. The knowledge of God doesn't just come; you seek for it, as King Solomon did. The knowledge of God tells you to praise God, and as you praise him, joy fills your heart, and his strength revitalizes you.

You will show me the path of life; In Your presence is fullness of joy; At Your right hand are pleasures forevermore. Psalm 16:11.

Joy is the outflow of God's presence, and the end product of joy is the release of strength. You cannot go to God with your weakness and return weak. You need to master the act of staying with God in prayer, studying God's word, and rendering praise to God always. As you do, there is a level of joy that replaces your sorrow, and when this happens, you are strengthened from within.

According to how we started our discussion here, your inner (spiritual) strength is what sustains other forces in your life.

No wonder Paul the Apostle prayed for fellow believers:

That He would grant you, according to the riches of His glory, to be strengthened with might through His Spirit in the inner man.

When you are weak in your inner man, you may feel like not praying, but that's actually what you need to do. Pray!

Prayer sustains and releases new strength to you. It is a lie from the pit of hell that you don't need to pray since you are in a difficult situation. When you rise to pray, you disappoint the devil and put the host of hell in panic. Rise, Christian soldier, don't give up!

Chapter 5

HE QUIETS MY SOUL

He restores my soul; He leads me in the paths of righteousness For His names sake. Psalm 23:3.

When the devil wants to attack, he goes directly to your soul. Not your spirit, because if you are a believer, your spirit man has been regenerated. However, your soul is being saved continually.

The devil has been on this battlefield for long, and he knows where to come in. He knows your soul is so tender, except you renew it continually. Your mind, being a compartment of your soul, is the place of historic battle and contention with you. He tells you all manners of good but not true things. They may look appealing to you, but his words are not true. The Devil wants you to feel God has forsaken you in a difficult time, which is a lie. He does not have any other weapon than lies. That's why you need to know the truth of the Word to contend with him. When your soul is distraught, there is only one person to run to, God!

David understood this, he said:

He restores my soul; He leads me in the paths of righteousness For His names sake (Psalm 23:3).

He wrote this Psalm when he was faced with a battle with king Saul, who did all he could to capture David but all to no avail until David saw Saul's end and all he had. The same battle exists between you and the arch enemy, devil. You don't have to surrender by backing out.

The Lord restores your soul and leads you in the path of righteousness when you solely rely on God's strength. He will restore your soul through rest. He will restore you through peace of mind. This will only happen if you come unto him.

Come to Me, all you who labor and are heavy laden, and I will give you rest. Matthew 11:28.

You don't have to do it alone but trust God in your little way, and he will fill your soul with rest no matter how hard it may look like.

SPEAK TO YOUR SOUL

One of the ways you can quiet your soul from trouble is to speak to your soul. Your soul can hear the sound of your voice. Tell your soul what is happening and what shall become of you. It would respond by quietness. The trouble will find it's way out of it.

Why are you cast down, O my soul? And why are you disquieted within me? Hope in God, for I shall yet praise Him For the help of His countenance. Psalm 42:5.

Words are so sharp and powerful that it can penetrate the deepest part of your soul and spirit. Use the Word of God to speak to your soul.

For the word of God is living and powerful, and sharper than any two-edged sword, piercing even to the division of soul and spirit, and of joints and marrow, and is a discerner of the thoughts and intents of the heart. Hebrew 4:12

The only thing that can enter into your soul and divide to separate all thoughts that are good from the unfruitful ones is the Word of God. Permit the Word to do a quick work on you today. Speak to your soul.

Chapter 6

WHEN LIFE GETS HARD

And they made their lives bitter with hard bondage—in mortar, in brick, and in all manner of service in the field. All their service in which they made them serve was with rigor. Exodus 1:14.

There would be hard times in the journey of every man. How you deal with it and the lesson learned is of great importance. You will surely go through and come out successfully as God lives.

There was a time the children of Israel were going through a kind of difficult time; they could not contain it any longer, and had to cry to God for mercy. God showed up and delivered them out of the difficult situation. Your case is not difficult for God. No matter how hard it may be, it is nothing compared to what He has done in the past; he can do it again.

It's dangerous to look for another way apart from God's way to solve any life issue. You should know that the more challenging the problem you are going through, the bigger your testimony would be because when God comes in, everything will become easy, and your journey would be smooth. No situation is ever difficult for Him.

Behold, I am the Lord, the God of all flesh. Is there anything too hard for Me?
Jeremiah 32:27

The reason you are finding your problem so hard is because, you have not come to He that has all the solutions with Him. He has never failed, and yours would not be different.

WHAT TO DO WHEN LIFE GETS HARD?

When things look upside down and challenge opposes, Call on God, He will answer you. You don't need to do anything destructive. Wait for God to bless you so that you will increase without any sorrow.

Call to Me, and I will answer you, and show you great and mighty things, which you do not know. Jeremiah 33:3

God is waiting to hear your call today, He wants to listen to you anytime. Even before you start speaking, He has heard and ready to answer you. It is the Word of God.

Read the scripture:
It shall come to pass That before they call, I will answer; And while they are still speaking, I will hear. Isaiah 65:24.

When everything around you looks so stiff and gloomy, you have someone and somewhere to run; Jesus who lives forever. In the time of your distress, call upon Him and you shall see Him in manifestation.

In my distress I called upon the Lord, And cried out to my God; He heard my voice from His temple, And my cry entered His ears. 2 Samuel 22:7

Chapter 7

GOD'S LOVE IS ETERNAL

There are different kinds of love ranging from Eros, Phileo, and Agape. The best and the greatest love is Agape, which is unconditional love; The type of love God has for us. The beautiful thing about this unconditional love is that it is eternal because God operates from eternity. God loves you, than you love yourself. There has never been a man who loves another like God.

Because God loves you, resting on him is easy. You can attest that there is no true lover who will not sacrifice for the other. Lovers go the extra mile to satisfy the want or needs of each other. In this case, you are in a love relationship with the best lover ever. The one who owns silver and gold whom the whole earth belongs to. What do you need that cannot be given unto you? What are your heart desires that He cannot give? Jesus asked, *"if you could give gift to your child whom you love how much more shall the Father give you your desire"*

If you then, being evil, know how to give good gifts to your children, how much more will your heavenly Father give the Holy Spirit to those who ask Him! Luke 11:30

You need to ask God what you want, don't assume. Ask what you want, pour your heart to the Father in love.

ASK ACCORDING TO HIS WILL

God has a WILL, which He will never
substitute for anything. As much as God
loves you, He will never lower His
standard for you, so you have to fit in into
His will and purpose.
There are times you ask if it's outside His
will; you cannot get it. God operates by
His own will, not your own will. The best
you can do is to find out His will
concerning what you desire and pray
accordingly.

The best way to pray accurately in God's
will is by praying in the spirit. Prayer in
tongues consistently if you have received
the baptism of the Holy Ghost, if you

have not then, you need to seek for this outpouring. The first asking God wants you to do so that you become accurate is to ask for the Holy Ghost's gift.

...How much more will your heavenly Father give the Holy Spirit to those who ask Him! Luke 11:30.

Ask for the Spirit because until the Spirit be poured upon you from on high, your desert would not become a forest.

Until the Spirit is poured upon us from on high, And the wilderness becomes a fruitful field, And the fruitful field is counted as a forest. Isaiah 32:15

It takes the Spirit of God to move from nothingness to something great. It takes the Spirit of God for you to be fruitful in life. As part of the love of God for mankind, He released the Spirit upon us. Lay hold on the promises of God for you by the Spirit today, ask for the fresh release of the Holy Spirit upon you.

Chapter 8

FEAR NOT

For God has not given us a spirit of fear, but of power and of love and of a sound mind. 2 Timothy 1:7

Fear is a torment. Part of what Jesus came to do in our time is to deliver us from fear. He destroyed the power of death over you to release you from fear.

And release those who through fear of death were all their lifetime subject to bondage. Hebrew 12:15.

You need not fear any longer. Jesus has paid for you. He paid with His blood and,

eventually, his death. So you need not
fear any longer.

Come into the knowledge of God for you
to overcome all your worries and fear.
Fear comes due to the absence of
knowledge; the more knowledge of the
kingdom of God, the bolder you become.
One of the reasons Jesus came is to
destroy the bondage of fear in us.

*For you did not receive the spirit of
bondage again to fear, but you received
the Spirit of adoption by whom we cry
out, Abba, Father. Romans 8:15.*
You have been delivered from fear, and
you need not have that fear any longer.
Instead of fear, you have been given the
spirit of adoption, which is the Spirit of
God. You can now call God your Father.

In times of trouble, you can call on Him.
He has given you power over your fear.
Whatsoever brings fear into your life can
be subdued by the Word of His power.

The reason you need not fear is that God
is with you. It is one thing for God to be
with a man, but the most important is for
you to know and be conscious of it every
time. How aware of his presence will
determine how much the situation will
bow before you. Mountains bow before
you at the appearance of God's presence.

God does not want you to fear anything
other than Him. In the case of God's fear,
we talk about the Holy reverence of God.
It is all about worship and obedience to
God's Word.

FEAR IS A MIRAGE

During a hot weather, the air can create a demonstration of an entity like water in certain areas. If you don't move close, you would actually think there is water in that part, but you will discover it is not on getting there.

This is how your fear operates. What you fear most is not real. It does not exist, but in your mind, that's why you have to deal with fear so it does not become your reality. What is that thing you have believed for a long time, bringing pain, sorrow, and hardship to you? You can do away with it now. It is not real. Your life is too precious to be held down by that fear.

Chapter 9

YOU ARE NOT ALONE

Fear not, for I am with you; Be not dismayed, for I am your God. I will strengthen you, Yes, I will help you, I will uphold you with My righteous right hand. Isaiah 41:10

You are assured by the scripture that you are not alone. God is ever for you and with you. This is the most valuable and essential thing in this world that God is with you always. It shows how precious you are to Him as long as you are his child. Indeed, God so loves the world, but there is a special preference for those who believe and obey Him.

The presence of God with you brings boldness and confers protection on you. It is good for you to know that the presence of God also makes provision available unto you. You may think if God is with me and His presence brings all these things, why am I still going through difficulty getting my needs. The reason is that all things are working out for your good. Surely, good things come from the Father.

Every good gift and every perfect gift is from above, and comes down from the Father of lights, with whom there is no variation or shadow of turning. James 1:17

Sometimes for you to get these gifts of the Father, you have to go through some process so that you would be a good custodian of the gift to the glory of God when you get it.

You may need to go through "winepress". At the winepress, the fruit is being pressed to get the best out of it, the juice. The more squeezing, the more the juice. So if you are going through any challenge or difficulty whatsoever, know that it is not as though God left you, but it's working for your good.

And we know that all things work together for good to those who love God, to those who are the called according to His purpose. Roman 8:28

As long as the Lord is your Father and you are walking with Him, they will all work for your good no matter what you are going through.

GOD IS ALWAYS NEAR

He is nearer than you can imagine. He is closer more than you can feel. God deeply resides in your spirit, and He lives in you. As long as you are one of His, you will see God working inside of you. No one can be as close to you as the Lord because He knows your inward part. You are a work of His hands.

God is close to you, but you will not see Him in action except you acknowledge

Him. You won't see His manifestation until you invoke Him in prayer and praise. A believer is always encouraged to pray because of the great potentials He carries within Him. He is instructed to pray so He can move the Lord who dwells inside of Him.

You cannot see the great possibilities of God except you are given to prayer. If you want to see God in action switch into prayer mode. The authentic power of God is generated in the praying process.

God does wonders in the life of those who believe He is near. Because by knowing He is with you, your faith will rise, and you will perform great works. The nearness of God to man can only be well felt and known through consistent and constant praying. This means you must live and breathe prayer.

If you have been praying consistently, you will soon touch God. Don't give up on Him; He is nearer than you think. Your dedication will be repaid. No matter how difficult a situation is, God is so close. Press on with determination. The proof that God is working with you will be Known to people who thought you were wasting your time. Jesus promised that He will be with you always.

Teaching them to observe all things that I have commanded you; and lo, I am with you always, even to the end of the age. Amen. Mathew 28:2.

Every Word of God is the truth and must be treated as such. God can never lie. It's very sure and certain. God said, I AM with you till the end of the world, meaning He is with you now, and He will forever be with you. You need to take advantage of this presence of God with man. You can invoke Him to your favor today. That situation that seems difficult is not, the devil only portrays that to you, to invoke your fear.

When a father is with his child, that child's confidence will soar to the high heavens. No one can come and beat a child where the father is, so also, you are God's child. So much price has been paid because of you. More than an earthly

Father will do for his child to protect him,
God will do for you.

Do you know that God can be in and with
you and the devil still finds a way around
you? The reason is because he wants to
hurt those that truly love and worship
God in spirit and truth. God will arise for
you as you invoke Him through your
prayer and praise today.

Chapter 10

FAITH OVER FEAR

Having faith is what gives you an edge over fear. Fear is from the devil. This is the reason God wants to eradicate fear. Fear is a limitation to those who have it.

For you did not receive the spirit of bondage again to fear, but you received the Spirit of adoption by whom we cry out, Abba, Father. Romans 8:15

The spirit of adoption from the father gives you boldness and paralyzes your fear. Knowing your father is enough to instill faith that will move mountains for you. The beautiful thing about faith is that, it will always win the battle over fear. Faith looks at fear face to face and breaks it down completely.

You have to nurture your faith to grow because your faith is the anchor of your destiny in Christ. No one else will build faith for you; it is your responsibility. You must be intentional about it. It will also interest you to know that the higher your faith, the stronger and higher your spiritual growth.

You cannot afford to joke with you're the growth of your faith. The more your faith, the more you enter into a place of rest because fear, which is the opposite of faith, brings unrest. God is so much interested in your faith; why? It gives Him a license for work in your life.

And often he has thrown him both into the fire and into the water to destroy him. But if You can do anything, have compassion on us and help us. Jesus said to him, if you can believe, all things are possible to him who believes. Mark 9:23-24.

It is not just about whether Jesus can do it or not. He can do all things, but do you believe He can? Your believing empowers him. It gives Him an avenue to work. If anyone believes a certain thing, the Lord is spurred to work on behalf of such a person to get it done, whichever means God wants to use.

HOW CAN I BUILD MY FAITH?

Through the Word:

So then faith comes by hearing, and hearing by the word of God.
Romans 10:17

Faith comes by hearing the Word of God and practicing it. As you listen to the Word consistently, your heart is enlarged by it and able to do exploits.

No word, no faith. As you behold Jesus through the Word, you begin to think and act like Him. That is the faith of God that comes by the Word.

*So Jesus answered and said to them,
Have faith in God. For assuredly, I say to
you, whoever says to this mountain, Be
removed and be cast into the sea, and I
say to you, whatever things you ask when
you pray, believe that you receive them,
and you will have them.*

You need faith to move mountains in
your life and around you. The Bible verse
above talked about having faith in God.
As you build up your faith by the word
that flows from His mouth, You also need
to speak to see your heart desires.

Through Prayer:
Prayer is important for building up your
faith; never stop praying because you have

not seen the result you desire. You have to continue in prayer if you have faith.

Therefore, I say to you, whatever things you ask when you pray, believe that you receive them, and you will have them. - Mark 11:24

The best and most accurate way to pray is in the Holy Ghost. It builds you up in your inner man to the point where your results will be eminent. There would be great proofs for your life and ministry.

But you, beloved, building yourselves up on your most holy faith, praying in the Holy Spirit, Jude 1:20

This build up is a continual exercise; you do not pray in the Holy Ghost because you want result, but because it is a communion language with God. It provides you rest in the Lord. Start praying in the Holy Ghost; do not stop because of anything. Make it your lifestyle.

REST IN GOD

Let us therefore be diligent to enter that rest, lest anyone fall according to the same example of disobedience. - Hebrew 4:11.

You are made for rest in God. That was the order from the beginning until sin came into the human race and the corresponding result was agony, pain, and suffering. It could have been much better and blissful than this for man if not for the fall of man.

The whole creation groans today simply because of this fall of man in Eden. Man has to go through rigor to make ends meet. Sometimes life becomes tiresome for the man that he thinks of death.

However, God has made room for our rest in Him. It takes your faith only to enter into this rest. Your faith gives you the license to rest in God. Without this rest, you will only be full of worries of life, which wearies the soul. Your soul would be full of anxiety and pain, except you take hold of the rest in God.

This rest is a place you have to enter. It has a key, and its door. The key is Faith. The children of Israel could not enter into God's rest because of unbelief. Unbelief is a serious yoke in the mind of God's because he would not be able to help us except we believe on Him; when you believe, God comes through to help you and you will enter into your rest.

For indeed the gospel was preached to us as well as to them; but the word which they heard did not profit them, not being mixed with faith in those who heard it. Hebrew 4:2.

The level of faith you have determines your rest, and when you rest in God, things happen in their own accord because you have trusted in the arm that made all things, not in the arm of human flesh like many persons in the world do.

Jesus gives rest, not the way it is in the world.

Peace I leave with you, My peace I give to you; not as the world gives do I give to you. Let not your heart be troubled, neither let it be afraid. John 14:27

In God, you get absolute peace and rest for your soul, not as the world. Let your mind be still waiting on God even when you have not gotten what you desire; your calmness in this situation depicts your rest in God.

Teaching them to observe all things that I have commanded you; and lo, I am with you always, even to the end of the age. Amen. Matthew 28:20

Chapter 11

GOD HAS A PLAN

God has a plan for you today, since the foundation of the world. He made you who you are by His will.

For I know the thoughts that I think toward you, says the Lord, thoughts of peace and not of evil, to give you a future and a hope. Jeremiah 29:11

Before you were even formed in the womb, the Lord knows you and has predetermined your destiny. He chose to allow you go through whichever process or dealings you are going through.

*Before I formed you in the womb I knew
you; Before you were born I sanctified
you; I ordained you a prophet to the
nations. Jeremiah 1:5.*

What you would become is known by
God; nothing is done without His
foreknowledge. Nothing happens without
His knowledge. Whatsoever you are
going through today is known unto God,
which should give you confidence that
your situation will turn around for joy.
There are times you go through
problems, which God allows in His
predetermined counsel for your rising
and becoming. If you do not go through,
you may not be able to achieve whatever
is in the mind of God for you in that
dispensation.

The devil, your arch-enemy may think he is oppressing you but behold, there is a wisdom behind it. If the devil had known, he would not have crucified Jesus. The crucifixion of Jesus led to the destruction of the devil. Worry no more because of your present challenge, it's all going to turn out well for you because God has a plan for you.

Which none of the rulers of this age knew; for had they known, they would not have crucified the Lord of glory. 1 Corinthians 2:8

There is a thought in the heart of God before He formed you. God plans to give you a great future. The plan of God is to make you a light to the world. However, before you can fully become this, there has to be training for you. The surprising thing is that God can use anything or anyone, including the devil, to train you. You will agree with me that most trainings are not easy; they are times of pruning, breakings, and remolding. You just have to go through it for your perfection.

God is interested in your growth and becoming than the pain. So focus on your development and purpose for which you are going through by looking unto Jesus, the author, and finisher of your faith.

Looking unto Jesus, the author and finisher of our faith, who for the joy that was set before Him endured the cross, despising the shame, and has sat down at

the right hand of the throne of God.
Hebrew 12:2

When you look unto Jesus, you would be able to do the same thing Jesus did. He didn't focus on the cross but the end product of that cross. He practically endured the process because He knows there is a good plan from the heart of the Father concerning Him and all He went through. He knew there would be joy and light after the process. You need to think and act like Him as you behold Him through His Holy Word.

Chapter 12

NEVER GIVE UP

Though thy beginning was small, yet thy latter end should greatly increase Job 8:7

Challenges are part of life. Life is full of ups and downs. There are times life will throw you to the ground. There will also be times that what you are expecting will be delayed, but one thing is associated with every successful person in life, and that is they never give up.

Never give up on your goals and plans in life. What you intend to achieve in life will pass through tough times but never give up. The best is yet to come.

There are certain areas of your life you should never give up. Few of them are discussed below.

1. Spiritually: Quite a number of Christians give up so soon in their work with God when their request or petition is not met.

This one thing every Christian must know is that patience is needed in this kingdom. Spiritually you must not give up. Observing your daily devotional, praying, and fasting may not be easy, but yet don't give up. Keep doing it. If it just a few minutes you can spend in God's presence, keep doing it. Don't ever give up

2. In fulfilling your dreams and purpose in life: Some people in life, when they notice their goals are not showing forth the way they expected, they tend to give up.

No matter the challenges you face in fulfilling your dreams, don't ever give up. Keep pursuing that goal. One day you will achieve it. Giving up will never solve the problem. So why give up?

In fulfilling your dreams, you need to keep focus and be determined. Every successful person never gave up on their dreams.

3. Marriage: Many people in our society have given up on their marriages. Married people are fed up already. That's why you

will see marriages of less than a year over.
Why? Because they gave up too soon.
There are challenges in every marriage.
Marriage is not going to smooth all year
out; there will be quarrels among the
couples, but that's not a license to give up.
Never give up on your spouse; better days
are ahead you. Today may look rough,
but tomorrow will be better.

Likewise, those who are of marriageable
age should not as well give up. That
partner will come. God never disappoints
His children. Delay is not denial. God
can still work out that marriage for your
good.

*In Roman 8:28, the scripture says "And
we know that all things work together for*

good to them that love God, to them who are the called according to his purpose."

Therefore, don't give up yet on your marital life. You can still get married to the person who will love you as God loves you.

And also, to those who are married and yet no childbirth, God will still make you laugh. Just as He did it for Sarah, Rebecca, and Rachel, He can do it for you.

Don't give up on God; the best is yet to come on your way. Giving up will not solve the problem, neither will it provide the solution. So put all your totality to God, and in due season, He will lift you up.

4 Financially: This is the most important aspect where people, even believers in particular tend to give up due to their financial woes. They give up due to lack of funds or inability to make ends meet. The economy of your country may not be favorable but yet keep trusting God. He can bring out the best from you.

In the scripture, there was famine and financial hardships in the land where Isaac dwelt. He wanted to leave the land and sort out himself, but God spoke to him in verse six of Genesis chapter twenty-six to dwell in Gerar.

"And Issac dwell in Gerar"Genesis 26:6

Isaac was about giving up in the areas of finance, but God suddenly showed up and gave him an instruction. He obeyed God and the result was amazing.

"And Issac sow in that land, and received in the same year an hundredfold: and the Lord blessed him" Genesis 26:12

Financially, don't give up. God can make a great thing to happen to you. He can make that business deal possible; He can revive your business once again. Never give up, because prosperity is on its way.

In conclusion, giving up will not solve the problem but rather worsen the situation. So why give up. Put in your best and involve God in that situation, and I'm sure

you will see success and incredible things
happening to you.

Chapter 13

WHEN YOU PRAISE HIM, HE WILL
RAISE YOU

The Lord opens the eyes of the blind;
The Lord raises those who are bowed
down; The Lord loves the righteous.
Psalm 146:8

What raises a man in life is praise not
complaint. Grumbling over certain things
in your life will never provide a solution.
Praise is what raises a man. Praise is that
solution.

There is power in worshipping God.
Worshipping him gives you assurance
and peace of mind over certain issues in
your life.
Praising God is what he desires from you.
Praise Him in the morning, afternoon
and night. Don't allow the challenges of
this life weight you down or stop you
from praising God.

If you must see the hand of God in
certain dimensions, then you must be
praiseful. God inhabits the praise of His
people. What God needs from you is
absolute devotion.

**WHAT PRAISING HIM WILL DO IN
YOUR LIFE**

Praise can give you the victory you so desire. Those who cultivate the habit of praising God tend to be victorious in all their endeavors.

Praise can deliver you from your enemies.

Praise commands God's attention, blessings and presence.

Praise enables God to stand by you and arise for your sake.

Praising God with the whole of your heart is what matters. You don't need anyone to leash you into the atmosphere of praise. Let praising God come and flow through you.

Do you aspire to be lifted and be elevated in life? If Yes, then you need to cultivate the lifestyle of worshipping God.

In Psalm 145:3-4, David acknowledges that a generation shall praise the work of God and shall declare His mighty hand. The desire of man on Earth should be that he would praise God always. The Psalmist says in *Psalm 107:8 that "Oh that men would praise the Lord for His goodness and for His wonderful works to the children of men"*

Praising God is for your benefit and not God alone. If you refuse to praise Him, He will remain God. if men refuse to praise God, He will raise stones to praise Him. God deserves your praise.

The food of God is your praise, so when you worship Him, He will raise you.

Divine lifting is embedded in praising God.

The secret of David was praise. The strength of David lies in his adoration. David was able to touch God because He was a man of praise. A man who worships God will always see the hand of God in his life.

No wonder David was lifted above all his enemies. Why? He was a man who adored God.

How can you praise God?

1. By dancing to his praise and worship
2. By singing songs that glorify his holy name

When it comes to praising God, you need to be humble. Praising God requires

humility. A proud man cannot praise
God.

Some Kings tried it, and their end was not
good at all. King Nebuchadnezzar praised
himself, and he was in the bush for good
seven years eating and dining with
animals.

Don't be full of yourself by taking the
place of God in your life. No matter what
your achievement is in life, keep praising
God. It is in praising God that you will be
lifted.

Finally, Jesus said in the book of St John
that *"If I be lifted up, will draw all men."*
When you lift the name of God high by
praising Him, He attends to you and
draws all things toward you.

Praising God is for your benefit. Stop the
complaints. Stop murmuring. Start

praising God, and see you lifting around
the corner.

Chapter 14

THE SITUATION IS TO YOUR ADVANTAGE

There's a purpose for everything that happens in life. Nothing good comes so easy. Every great people make use of the opportunity that comes their way.

The current situation you are in right now can still work out for your good. You can still achieve your goals and dreams.

You probably have great ambition for yourself. You have seen your self be a great person in life. And you have a vision of yourself being successful, but the situation you are presently is not favorable.

I have good news for you today. That situation is to your advantage. You can bring out the best in that situation.

There was a time people thought nothing good could come out from Nazareth. But Jesus proved them wrong.

You don't need to give up or keep fighting those around your vicinity. All you need is to work on yourself and bring out the best from that situation.

The way you see that particular situation in your life will determine whether the problem is for your advantage. If you see success, you will end that situation in success.

The situation you are facing right now is for your advantage. *Roman 8:28 says all things work for good to them that love*

God. If you're in Christ, no problem can overwhelm you because you know he is by your side and he will not give you a cross you cannot carry.

However, for anything to work for your good or be to your advantage, you need to have the right mindset. No matter how bad what you're facing right now, have positive motives and reaction toward that situation

We have an assurance in Christ that all things will work out well for us. Nevertheless, there is a role believers need to play in making those situations work out well. Such roles are:

1. Positive affirmation: Keep speaking positive things to that

situation. Stop saying negative
words that will weigh you down.
The situation is to your advantage.

2. Positive mindset: Your mindset
    toward a situation should be
    positive.

3. Positive Attitude and reaction:
    your reaction and attitude toward a
    particular situation has a role to
    play. How do you react toward a
    problem or what is your attitude
    towards a problem? If you want
    your situation to work for your
    good or your advantage, you need
    to be positive always

Chapter 15

IT SPEAKS AT THE END

Prov.23.18 - For surely there is an end; and thine expectation shall not be cut off.

Today, may look as if you're nobody, but tomorrow will speak for itself. There is a future after today. Yesterday is your past, today is your present, and tomorrow is your future.

What you are today may not speak particular results in your life, but the end shall tell of Gods glory in your life.

The scripture says *"Eccl.7.8- Better is the end of a thing than the beginning thereof:"* The end has a voice that speaks faster and better than the beginning. At first, your business may not yield profit at first, or your spiritual growth may not be productive at first. At first, you may not have produced certain results in your life, but the future is better.

Your beginning doesn't matter but the end does. It is the end that justifies the means. If you don't relent and give up, the future will be productive.
You pray for the sick, and nothing happens. You fast and pray for three days and the situation still looks so impossible. Don't worry, the end is going to be better. With your consistency and perseverance, you will attain that which you desire through Christ Jesus.

Keep speaking good towards your end. The days of your struggles is coming to an end soon. Weeping may endure all night, but joy comes in the morning. That's the assurance God gave to us. Suffering and struggling in any area of your life is not for a lifetime. There is an expiry time allocated to it.

Stop worrying about life, it is only God who can determine a man's end. Without God, the end of a man is miserable. You need to depend on God to make your end a better one.

Factors to have a better end

1. God: You can't neglect the place of God in fulfilling your destiny. You

need to trust God if you must have a beautiful ending in this life. Your beginning doesn't matter; what matters is your ending. And it is only God who knows the ending from the beginning. So trust Him for a beautiful ending.

2. Focus: This will help you to have a better ending. Never lose your focus. Never look down on your small beginning. The end is amazing. Let your direction be right and straight. Do not be distracted. Do not allow evil people to have a say in your life. Keep focusing on your life, and your ending will speak for itself.

3. Determination: This is a key factor in becoming great. How determined are you in achieving your dream and reaching your goals in life?

4. Commitment: Anything that is valuable needs total commitment. You need to be committed in what you are doing if you must finish well. Responsibility is what will lead you to succeed in the end.

5. Humility: God resists the proud but giveth grace to the humble. With humility, you can reach the top. The end you are expecting will occur as a result of your

humility toward God and man.
Have respect for God and man.

6. Perseverance: One secret of being great is the ability to persevere. It is a virtue you must have to reach the top. It's not going to be easy along the way, but with perseverance, you can get the top and have a glorious ending.

Today is the reflection of your future. Your ending is determined by what you are doing today. Greater heights are awaiting you at the end if only you can maximize your beginning well.

A RENEWED STRENGTH

Isa.40.31 - But they that wait upon the LORD shall renew their strength; they shall mount up with wings as eagles; they shall run, and not be weary; and they shall walk, and not faint.

Strength is necessary to carry out a routine. Without strength a man can fall and even fail.

The Bible says when you fail in the days of your adversary they strength is fall.

It takes a man who is strengthened to stand and be energetic. Strength is needed in everyday activities, be it spiritually, physically, mentally, and health-wise.

You need to know that as a Christian, your strength needs to be renewed. When talking about renewing strength, we need to note that only God can give such strength with the Holy Ghost's help.

"For by man strength shall no man prevail".-1 Samuel 2:9

You can't prevail in the journey of life with your human strength. You can fail, but the strength that comes from God renews your body, soul and spirit. Everyone has to come to the point of relying on God's strength which is renewed every day. When God strength is placed on your life, things won't be hard for you.

*Isa.40.29 - He giveth power to the faint;
and to them that have no might he
increaseth strength.*

God is the only one who can give strength
to a man. Those who are faint can seek
out strength from God. You need to trust
God for divine strength in your daily
activities and your life entirely.

*Isa.40.30 - Even the youths shall faint and
be weary, and the young men shall utterly
fall*

There are biblical characters we need to
example. We will examine just two out of
many

1. Elijah: As powerful as Elijah was, he was weary, fed up, and tired. His strength failed him, but a supernatural strength was released on him when he relied on God. His power was renewed by eating the food provision made available for him.

1Kings.19.4 - But he himself went a day's journey into the wilderness, and came and sat down under a juniper tree: and he requested for himself that he might die; and said, It is enough; now, O LORD, take away my life; for I am not better than my fathers.

Imagine a great man of God getting weary. The strength needed is no longer available. The only option he thought of was death. This is a lesson to young people and ministers of the Gospel that you can't serve God with your strength. Your strength will fail you.

You need the strength of God. With Elijah's strength renewed, he went to Mount Horeb for forty days and forty nights.

1Kings.19.8 - And he arose, and did eat and drink, and went in the strength of that meat forty days and forty nights unto Horeb the mount of God.

As a minister of God, you need the new strength of the Holy Ghost to carry you through. It is not by power neither by might but by the strength of God be made available.

2. Samson: Samson was a powerful man simply because God's strength was made available in his life. The power of Samson was not ordinary but supernatural. He was so powerful, the strength of killing a lion was rested upon him.

Judg.14.5 - Then went Samson down, and his father and his mother, to Timnath, and came to the vineyards of Timnath: and, behold, a young lion roared against him.

It only takes supernatural strength for a man to kill a lion without any physical weapon.

The strength of God can make one victorious.

Judg.14.6 - And the Spirit of the LORD came mightily upon him, and he rent him as he would have rent a kid, and he had nothing in his hand: but he told not his father or his mother what he had done.

How can I renew my strength?

Isa.40.31 - But they that wait upon the LORD shall renew their strength; they shall mount up with wings as eagles; they shall run, and not be weary; and they shall walk, and not faint.

To renew your strength, you need to wait upon God in prayer, in studying the

Word, fasting, and in the secret place of the most high.

In conclusion, your strength will fail you. Rely on God to renew your strength day by day.

A Prayer for Hard Times

Lord, I thank You for You are the God and Lord of the entire universe; the God who makes all things possible. You are mighty, powerful, righteous and true. I want to trust in Your ability and not my own. Help me to see difficulties in my life as trials to overcome with you by my side. Just as your son carried his cross and was glorified, Lord help me to carry the crosses this life bestows upon me.

Teach me to focus on You and Your power even in hard circumstances when my strength and faith might be failing. Help me to read, trust, and obey Your Word. Today I bring before You this difficulty in my life **[Name a tough situation you are in right now]**. I commit this situation in your hand for I know with you I can surmount all difficulties. Help me not to fear but to put my trust You in you. I declare my faith in Your ability and know you will fight for me and win the battles in my life. I will be strong and courageous even in hard times for I have nothing to fear with You by my side. I will not be terrified or discouraged, for I know you will be with me wherever I go

Lord please Show me Your mercy; show me your supernatural power. Teach me how to walk by faith and pray breakthrough prayers. Grant me patience, and faith that through You I have already more than conquered, confidence that these times will pass in Your own good time, and expectant joy that I will live with You forever. Amen.

Printed in Great Britain
by Amazon

73601876R00068